In 1907, 20-year-old Diego Rivera traveled across the Atlantic Ocean to Europe for the first time.

TIMELINE OF DIEGO RIVERA'S LIFE

1886 Diego Rivera is born in Guanajuato, Mexico.

1892 The Rivera family moves to Mexico City, the capital of Mexico.

1896 During grade school, Diego takes night classes at the San Carlos School of Fine Arts. Two years later, he starts attending the school full-time.

1907 Diego wins an art scholarship and travels to Europe.

1921 After studying art and meeting many soon-to-be-famous artists in Europe, Diego returns to Mexico.

1922 Diego paints his first mural in Mexico City. You can see that painting on pages 20 and 21 of this book.

1929 Diego Rivera marries Frida Kahlo. Frida soon becomes a famous artist, too.

THIS WAY

UP HERE

1930 Diego and Frida are invited to the United States. Over the next three years, Diego paints murals in San Francisco, Detroit, and New York City. Wealthy people, movie stars, and government officials enjoy throwing parties for the popular couple.

1947 Diego keeps very busy creating dozens of large murals in public areas. He wants everyone to see them, enjoy them, and learn about the history of their country.

1954 Frida Kahlo dies.

1955 Diego donates his historical art collection and his house as a museum for the people of Mexico.

1957 Diego Rivera dies in Mexico City at the age of 70.

GETTING TO KNOW THE WORLD'S GREATEST ARTISTS

DIEGO RIVERA

WRITTEN AND ILLUSTRATED BY MIKE VENEZIA

CONSULTANT MEG MOSS

CHILDREN'S PRESS®

An Imprint of Scholastic Inc.

To the kids at St. Pius X School.

Cover: *Diego Rivera, The Flower Carrier, 1935, oil and tempera on Masonite; 48 in. x 47 3/4 in.; San Francisco Museum of Modern Art, Albert M. Bender Collection, gift of Albert M. Bender in memory of Caroline Walter/© 2015 Banco de México Diego Rivera & Frida Kahlo Museums Trust, Mexico, D.F./Artists Rights Society (ARS), New York, photo Ben Blackwell*

© 2015 Banco de México Diego Rivera & Frida Kahlo Museums Trust, Mexico, D.F./Artists Rights Society (ARS), New York

Library of Congress Cataloging-in-Publication Data

Venezia, Mike.
  Diego Rivera / by Mike Venezia. – Revised Edition.
    pages cm. – (Getting to know the world's greatest artists)
  Includes bibliographical references and index.
  ISBN 978-0-531-21261-5 (library binding : alk. paper) – ISBN 978-0-531-21323-0 (pbk. : alk. paper) 1. Rivera, Diego, 1886-1957–Juvenile literature.
2. Artists–Mexico–Biography–Juvenile literature. I. Title.

  N6559.R58V45 2015
  759.972–dc23
  [B]

2015020969

1 2 3 4 5 6 7 8 9 10 R 25 24 23 22 21 20 19 18 17 16

Self Portrait,
by Diego Rivera.
1941. Oil on canvas,
24 x 16 7/8 inches.
Smith College
Museum of Art,
Northampton,
Massachusetts.
Gift of Irene Rich
Clifford, 1977.

Diego Rivera thought it was important to make paintings for everyday working people to enjoy. He hoped his art would teach people about their past and give them hope for the future.

To make it easier for lots of people to see his artwork, Diego Rivera painted huge pictures called *murals* on the walls of schools, churches, hospitals, hotels, and government buildings. Diego usually painted on wet plaster with watercolors, a technique known as fresco painting.

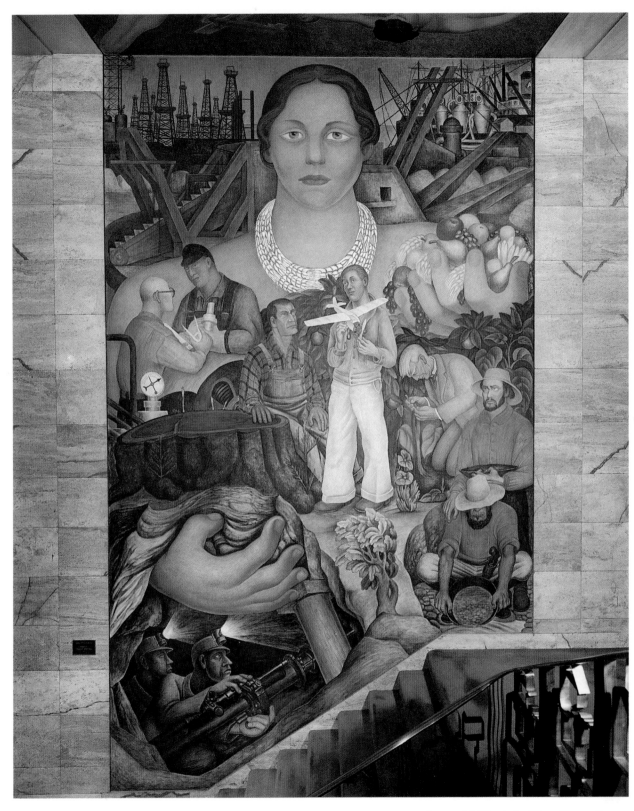

Allegory of California, by Diego Rivera. Fresco,
471.69 square feet. Pacific Stock Exchange,
San Francisco, California. Photograph © Dirk Bakker.

Diego was a great storyteller. His paintings usually tell a story about the history of Mexico, or people at work, or how something is made. In *The Making of a Fresco*, Diego showed himself and his assistants painting a mural. He also showed sculptors, and engineers and architects planning new buildings. Some people became upset when they saw that Diego had painted himself with his backside to them. They thought he was being rude. Diego Rivera often upset people with his work.

The Making of a Fresco Showing the Building of a City, by Diego Rivera. April-June, 1931. Fresco, 22 feet 7 inches x 29 feet 9 inches. San Francisco Art Institute. Photograph © David Wakely.

Diego Rivera was born in 1886 in the Mexican town of Guanajuato. He always had a wonderful imagination. When he was very young, he spent lots of time in the Mexican forest with his pet goat. He said he made friends with all the animals there, even the dangerous and poisonous ones.

When he was a little older, Diego
started to draw. He particularly loved
to draw inventions that he made up
in his head, and the mechanical parts
of toys he took apart. Diego drew on

anything he could find—even the walls! This became such a problem that his father decided to cover a whole room for him with canvas in order to save the rest of the house.

When he was ten years old, Diego decided he wanted to become an artist. Because he was an excellent student (and very stubborn once he made up his mind), his parents sent him to the famous San Carlos art academy in Mexico City. Diego's teachers taught him to draw and paint. They also taught him all the important things they had learned from the great artists of Spain, France, and Italy.

Satire on the comet that appeared in 1899.
Reproduced from *Posada's Popular Mexican
Prints*, published by Dover Publications, Inc.

Diego said he learned about the art
of his own country from a teacher he
found all by himself. José Posada
owned a small printing shop near the
academy. Diego would often stop by
to watch Posada make his drawings
and prints.

Diego had never seen anything like Posada's pictures of Mexican legends and everyday events. He thought Posada's drawings were so full of energy and life that they might jump off the page at any moment.

The Grinder, by Diego Rivera. 1924.
Encaustic on canvas, 35 $^4/_{10}$ x 46 inches.
Museo de Arte Moderno, Mexico City, Mexico.
Photograph © Dirk Bakker.

Years later, Diego too would
paint scenes of everyday events.

Woman at the Well, by Diego Rivera. 1913. Oil on canvas, 56 6/10 x 52 3/10 inches. Museo Nacional de Arte, Mexico City, Mexico. Photograph © Dirk Bakker.

While Diego was growing up, Mexico's government wasn't working very well. Few people in Mexico had enough money to be able to enjoy themselves, and hardly anyone knew how to read. Diego saw that many people in Mexico were living almost like slaves. It bothered him very much.

In 1907, when Diego was twenty, he went to study art in Europe. There he became friends with artists who were already famous, like Pablo Picasso and Amedeo Modigliani. Diego was influenced by these artists. Soon, he started to become known for his own paintings. Some of them looked very much like Pablo Picasso's cubist paintings.

Untitled (Man with a Mustache, Buttoned Vest and Pipe, Seated in an Armchair), by Pablo Picasso. 1915. Oil on canvas, 51 ^{2}/10 x 35 ^{2}/10 inches. Gift of Mrs. Leigh B. Block in memory of Albert D. Lasker, 1952.1116. Photograph © 1994, The Art Institute of Chicago. All rights reserved.

Even though Diego Rivera was doing well in Europe, he felt that something was missing from his art. Diego worried that his paintings were being enjoyed only by well-educated people who were wealthy enough to buy them for their homes. He thought that art should be enjoyed by everyone—especially poor, working people.

While on a trip to Italy, Diego saw frescoes that had been painted hundreds of years earlier.

Flight into Egypt, by Giotto. Fresco, 72 $^8/_{10}$ x 78 $^7/_{10}$ inches. Scrovegni Chapel, Padua, Italy. Scala / Art Resource, NY.

Usually, these were painted on the walls of churches (like the one above), so everyone in a town or city could enjoy them. Diego decided he would return to Mexico to make paintings for all the people there to enjoy.

When Diego arrived in Mexico, he was asked to paint a large mural for an important school. Diego named the painting *Creation*.

People all over Mexico thought it was wonderful! They loved the beautiful, rich colors; the strong, solid shapes of the people; and the skillful way Diego had made the painting fit into the space of the building.

Creation, by Diego Rivera. 1922-23. Fresco, encaustic and gold leaf, 23 2/10 x 39 3/10 feet. Escuela Nacional Preparatoria, Anfiteatro Bolivar, Mexico City, Mexico. Photograph © Dirk Bakker.

Detail of *For the Complete Safety of All Mexicans at Work: The Harvest,* by David Alfaro Siqueiros. 1952-54. Mural. Hospital de la Raza, Mexico City, Mexico. Schalkwijk/Art Resource, NY.

Diego was soon given more jobs. He worked hard to get away from his European influences and create a style of art that was all his own. He especially wanted to make art that was more Mexican in feeling. Other artists also began painting murals at this time. David Siqueiros and José

Detail of *The Working Class,* by José Clemente Orozco. 1923-27. Mural. Escuela Nacional Preparatoria San Ildefonso, Mexico City, Mexico. Schalkwijk/Art Resource, NY.

Clemente Orozco were two other
Mexican artists who became famous
for their beautiful and powerful
works. It seemed like murals were
popping up all over Mexico.

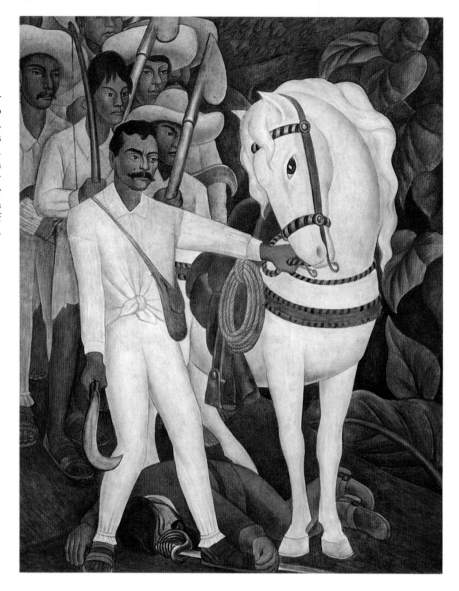

Diego often painted revolutionary events and the leaders who were fighting to change things in Mexico so people would have more rights and freedom. Some people, though,

thought things in Mexico were just fine the way they were. They sometimes became angry at what the mural artists were showing, and would throw rocks at the artists and their work! Diego decided to arm himself for protection.

During the 1930s, Diego Rivera was invited to paint murals in the United States. One of the most famous was called *Detroit Industry*. Diego painted it on the walls of a large room in the art museum in Detroit, Michigan.

Detroit Industry, South Wall, by Diego Rivera. 1932-33. Mural. © The Detroit Institute of Arts, Founders Society Purchase, Edsel B. Ford Fund and Gift of Edsel B. Ford.

In one section of *Detroit Industry*, Diego showed factory workers making steel and engine parts for cars. Diego saw beauty in modern machinery as well as in people. He gave his mural lots of life by making

a conveyor belt move through the huge
factory almost like a snake. Fire from
the open furnace and the giant machines
remind some people of Indian gods at
an ancient Mexican ceremony.

Diego Rivera lived to be seventy years old, and had a very exciting life. He and his wife, Frida Kahlo, who was also a famous artist, attracted attention wherever they went.

Diego Rivera working on a mural in 1950. Courtesy of The Detroit Institute of Arts.

Frida and Diego Rivera, by Frida Kahlo. 1931. Oil on canvas, 39 3/8 x 31 inches. San Francisco Museum of Modern Art, San Francisco, California. Albert M. Bender Collection, Gift of Albert M. Bender.

Sometimes people didn't like what Diego showed in his paintings. One of Diego's murals in the United States was torn off the wall after Diego insisted on showing a portrait of a Russian revolutionary leader who was unpopular in America at the time.

Diego always painted what he felt was important, no matter what anyone thought.

Detail of *Man, Controller of the Universe*, by Diego Rivera. 1934. Fresco, 15 $^9/_{10}$ x 37 $^6/_{10}$ feet. Museo de Palacio de Bellas Artes, Mexico City, Mexico City. Photograph © Dirk Bakker.

It was especially important to him to show the history and beauty of the Mexican people he loved so much.

Flower Day, by Diego Rivera. 1925. Oil on canvas, 58 x 47 $^1/_2$ inches. Los Angeles County Museum of Art, Los Angeles County Funds.

The History of Medicine in Mexico: The People's Demand for Better Health, by Diego Rivera. 1953. Hospital de la Raza, Mexico City, Mexico. Photograph © Dirk Bakker.

Most of Diego Rivera's murals are in Mexico, but a few are in the United States. If you get a chance to see one, you'll notice how well it fits into the design of the building. Diego thought a lot about the architecture of a building before starting to paint.

The works of art in this book came from:
The Art Institute of Chicago
Escuela Nacional Preparatoria Anfiteatro Bolivar, Mexico City, Mexico
Founders Society Detroit Institute of Art, Detroit, Michigan
Hospital de la Raza, Mexico City, Mexico
Los Angeles County Museum of Art, Los Angeles, California
Museo de Arte Moderno, Mexico City, Mexico
Museo de Palacio de Bellas Artes, Mexico City, Mexico
Museo Nacional de Arte, Mexico City, Mexico
The Museum of Modern Art, New York, New York
Pacific Stock Exchange, San Francisco, California
Palacio Nacional, Mexico City, Mexico
San Francisco Art Institute, San Francisco, California
San Francisco Museum of Modern Art, San Francisco, California
Smith College Museum of Art, Northampton, Massachusetts
Scrovegni Chapel, Padua, Italy
Universidad Autonoma de Chapingo, Chapingo, Mexico